YOUR KNOWLEDGE HAS VALUE

Bibliographic information published by the German National Library:

The German National Library lists this publication in the National Bibliography; detailed bibliographic data are available on the Internet at http://dnb.dnb.de .

Imprint:

Copyright © 2019 GRIN Verlag
Print and binding: Books on Demand GmbH, Norderstedt Germany
ISBN: 9783346038906

This book at GRIN:

https://www.grin.com/document/500483

Kenneth Bacala

English for Specific Purposes in the Senior High School Curriculum

GRIN Verlag

GRIN - Your knowledge has value

Since its foundation in 1998, GRIN has specialized in publishing academic texts by students, college teachers and other academics as e-book and printed book. The website www.grin.com is an ideal platform for presenting term papers, final papers, scientific essays, dissertations and specialist books.

Visit us on the internet:

http://www.grin.com/

http://www.facebook.com/grincom

http://www.twitter.com/grin_com

ENGLISH FOR SPECIFIC PURPOSES IN THE SENIOR HIGH SCHOOL CURRICULUM

Kenneth G. Bacala
Recoletos de Bacolod Graduate School
University of Negros Occidental – Recoletos
Bacolod City

ABSTRACT

This descriptive research examined the extent of application of English for Specific Purposes (ESP) in the English for Academic and Professional Purposes (EAPP) curriculum for Grade 12 students in the public schools in the Municipality of Binalbagan, Negros Occidental. The participants of the study were the 233 Grade 12 students who were enrolled during the second semester of the school year 2017-2018. The quantitative descriptive design was utilized to determine the extent of application of ESP in the EAPP curriculum. The results revealed a high extent of application of ESP in the EAPP curriculum for Grade 12 students, however, when they were grouped according to each strand, HE and HUMSS were of the very high extent while GAS, IA, and AFA were of the high extent. Meanwhile, when the strands were categorized to Content Standard (CS), ABM and HE were of the very high extent while HUMSS, GAS, IA, and AFA were of the high extent of application. Also, when the strands are categorized according to Performance Standard (PS), HUMSS and HE were of the very high extent while GAS, IA, and AFA were of the high extent. There were significant differences found among the strands and standards in the extent of application of ESP in the EAPP curriculum. Hence, the proposed training program for ESP is designed to enrich the knowledge and learning materials for the senior high school students and the English teachers based on the findings of the study.

Keywords: English for Aacademic Professional Purposes English for Specific Purposes, the extent of application, strands, content standard, performance standard

Table of Contents

INTRODUCTION

The use of language in various disciplines, whether in academics, profession and occupation, plays a flexible role to meet the needs of the specific group of learners for them to be active and proficient in their chosen tracks. English is a global language, and it has been the medium of communication of intercultural organizations and businesses, which makes its dominant use in classroom instruction imperative. The broad concept of English is used in specific fields and different situations in the world of business, science, and technology (Barnawi, 2011).

Antic (2016) defines English for Specific Purposes (ESP) as an approach to language teaching and learning that is based on the needs of the learners. Bracaj (2014) also states that learners study English in class not only as a requirement but also as a need to be able to perform tasks even outside the campus. Also, ESP is designed to be learned and practiced as the basic component in the preparation for employment or occupational mobility (Kuo, 2016). Hence, ESP is integrated into the English instruction to prepare students for target communicative situations in their future professions and business and industry.

The Republic Act 10533 states that the Department of Education [DepEd] (2013) shall formulate the design and details of the enhanced basic education curriculum. It shall work with the Commission on Higher Education (CHED) to craft harmonized basic and tertiary curricula for the global competitiveness of Filipino graduates. To ensure college readiness and to avoid remedial and duplication of primary education subjects, the DepEd shall coordinate with the CHED and the Technical Education and Skills Development Authority (TESDA).

However, the researcher has observed that the EAPP reader used as the learning material for the senior high school students have insufficiency on the contents. Thus, there is a need to enrich the application of ESP in the EAPP curriculum for the Grade 12 students of the public schools in the Municipality of Binalbagan by integrating the competencies from the purposive communication and by conducting a training program for developing strategic intervention materials for English teachers.

This study aimed to determine the extent of application of English for Specific Purposes in the English for Academic and Professional Purposes curriculum for Grade 12 students in the public schools in the Municipality of Binalbagan, Negros Occidental during the second semester of the School Year 2017-2018.

Specifically, the study sought to answer the following questions:

1. What is the extent of application of ESP in the EAPP curriculum for the senior high in the public schools of the Municipality of Binalbagan as assessed by the Grade 12 students as a whole and when their

2

assessment is categorized according to strands: General Academic Strand (GAS), Industrial Arts (IA), Accountancy and Business Management (ABM), Humanities and Social Sciences (HUMSS), Home Economics (HE), and Agri-Fishery Arts (AFA)?

2. What is the extent of application of ESP in the EAPP curriculum for the senior high in the public schools of the Municipality of Binalbagan when the assessment of the Grade 12 students is categorized according to standards: Content Standard (CS) and Performance Standard (PS)?

3. Is there a significant difference in the extent of application of ESP in the EAPP curriculum for the senior high in the public schools of the Municipality of Binalbagan as assessed by the Grade 12 students and when their assessment is categorized according to strands?

4. Is there a significant difference in the extent of application of English for Specific Purposes in the English for Academic and Professional Purposes curriculum for the senior high in the public schools of the Municipality of Binalbagan when the assessment of the Grade 12 students is categorized in terms of standards?

The following hypotheses were formulated in this study based on the previous statement of the problem:

1. There is no significant difference in the extent of application of ESP in the EAPP curriculum for the senior high in the public schools of the Municipality of Binalbagan as assessed by the Grade 12 students and when their assessment is grouped according to strands.

2. There is no significant difference in the extent of application of ESP in the EAPP curriculum for the senior high in the public schools of the

Municipality of Binalbagan when the assessment of the Grade 12 students is categorized in terms of standards.

The present study was anchored on Swales's Genre Analysis (1990), Miyake and Tremarco's Needs Analysis (2005), Chambers's Target Situation Analysis (1980), and Enhanced Basic Education Act (2013).

This study was concerned with the extent of application of ESP in EAPP curriculum as assessed by the Grade 12 students of the public schools in the Municipality of Binalbagan during the second semester of the Academic Year 2017-2018 when their assessment is grouped according to strands and standards. Further, this study used quantitative research design utilizing the descriptive method.

The results of this study are beneficial to the curriculum designers to develop lessons and activities needed by every strand that will prepare students for their chosen courses for the college years. At the same time, it may be the guide for the curriculum makers to include authentic and contextualized activities in medicine, business, academics, law, criminal education, tourism, and other fields.

Also, to the English Education Program Specialist (EEPS) to provide training for English teachers and to customize instructional materials in EAPP subject. Likewise, the results will use as the basis to conduct a needs assessment and to develop plans and programs for ESP teachers.

Likewise, to the school administrators to come up with a working committee that will give focus on designing and contextualizing the lessons and activities for EAPP subject. The results may be the basis for planning programs in school or in a community that will prepare students for their future professions.

Similarly, for the English teachers to initiate classroom-based activities and integrate lessons related to the chosen strand of the students. Likewise, the results shall be used by the English teachers to integrate the competencies of the purposive communication and to provide ESP materials based on the needs of the students through using differentiated resources as the springboard for the discussion.

Moreover, to the students to develop and enhance their communication skills in academe and activities related to their tracks.

Furthermore, to the stakeholders to collaborate with the senior high students especially to those strands which are aligned with their given work opportunity when the students will be deployed to their agency or company for training purposes.

Finally, to the researchers to conduct their future research work on the effectiveness of using ESP approach in English language learning.

For a thorough understanding of the study, the following terms are defined conceptually and operationally.

Curriculum refers to the knowledge and skills of the learners expected to learn. It includes the subjects and competencies needed to be studied and to have before graduation (SHS Student Primer, 2015). Operationally, this term refers to the subject, EAPP, offered to the Grade 12 students.

EAPP refers to the curriculum that is concerned with the two main areas. English for Academic Purposes which refers to students' academic needs and of matched professionals who would seek a career in the educational setting while English for Professional Purposes refers

to the actual needs of (future) professionals (Ypsilandis and Kantaridou, 2007 as cited in Ruiz-Garrido et al., 2010). Operationally, this term refers to the subject in the senior high school where ESP is applied.

ESP refers to the use of English (whether a second or foreign language) in the specific domain of teaching and learning process which is considered as the second and foreign language (Paltridge and Starfield, 2013). Operationally, this term refers to the approach used by the teachers in the English for Academic and Professional Purposes curriculum in the senior high school.

Senior High School refers to the last two years of the K-12 program and includes Grades 11 and 12. In SHS, students will go through a core curriculum and subjects under a track of their choice (Senior High School | Department of Education, n.d.).

Operationally, this term refers to the public schools in the Municipality of Binalbagan which were the participating schools in the study. These schools were the Binalbagan National High School, Payao National High School, Bi-ao National High School, and Binalbagan National High School – Negros Occidental School of Fishery (NOSOF) Extension.

Senior High School Student refers to the senior student in a high school who are the oldest and who have reached an advanced level in their studies (senior high school students definition | English dictionary for learners | Reverso, n.d.).

Standard is something against which other things are compared for the purpose of determining accuracy, estimating quantity or judging quality. It is a broadly stated expectation of what one should know and be able to do (www.officialgazette.gov.ph).

Strand refers to the specialized curricular offerings under a particular track (DO 32, s. 2016 - Addendum to DepEd Order No. 3, S. 2016 | Department of Education, n.d.). Operationally, strand refers to the offered specializations in senior high school in preparation for their college years or career. The following strands are the ABM, AFA, GAS, HE, HUMSS, and IA.

METHODOLOGY

This study employed the quantitative descriptive design to determine the extent of application of ESP in the EAPP curriculum for the senior high in the public schools of the Municipality of Binalbagan.

The participants of the study were the Grade 12 students who were officially enrolled in the School Year 2017-2018 at Binalbagan National High School, Payao National High School, Bi-ao National High School and Binalbagan National High School – Negros Occidental School of Fishery (NOSOF) Extension. To determine the samples of the study, the Stratified Random Sampling was used by utilizing the Raosoft sample size calculator. Out of 596 senior high school (SHS) students, only 233 SHS students were the samples of the study.

A researcher-made questionnaire was used and composed of two parts: Part I focused on the content standard and Part II comprised of performance standard that reflected the extent of application of ESP in the EAPP curriculum.

To establish the validity of the test instrument, the researcher submitted it to the three jurors who were experts in their respective field and were requested to make corrections, suggestions, and recommendations for the improvement of the test instrument by using the Good and Scates validation form. Thus, the value of the validity index is 3.45 which means that the survey questionnaire is interpreted as Good.

To establish the reliability of the study, the test instrument was exposed to a pilot testing to the randomly chosen thirty (30) Grade 12 students of Binalbagan Catholic College – High School Department. After the administration of the test, the data were classified and subjected to Cronbach Alpha formula. Thus, the reliability rating is .897 which reveals that the instrument is reliable.

In gathering the data, the researcher sought the approval of the Dean of the Graduate School of the University of Negros Occidental – Recoletos de Bacolod to conduct the study. Then, a letter of approval was sent to the Schools Division Superintendent of the Division of Negros Occidental and Asst. Schools Division Superintendent, Officer-In-Charge of the Southern Negros. Also, the communication letters were sent to the respective school principals of the different public secondary schools in the municipality of Binalbagan to conduct and gather data from the Grade 12 students on the extent of application of ESP in the senior high school curriculum during the School Year 2017-2018. The researcher personally managed and utilized the self-administered questionnaire to the participants by instructing on how to accomplish the test. The gathered data were retrieved immediately and tabulated, analyzed, and interpreted by the researcher.

Moreover, this research study was conducted to the participants with the permission of the Schools Division

Superintendent of the Division of Negros Occidental, Officer-In-Charge - Assistant Schools Division Superintendent in the Southern Negros, school principals of the public schools in the Municipality of Binalbagan, and the Grade 12 students. This study took place in the Grade 12 classrooms within the regular settings and schedules. There was no remuneration involved and no instruction that can compromise the learners during the conduct of the study. Moreover, the data collected from the participants were disposed and kept confidentially after the completion and approval of the study.

This study used the descriptive and comparative schemes, and the data were analyzed using Statistical Package for the Social Sciences (SPSS) for statistical treatment. Meanwhile, the Mean and Standard Deviation were used in Problem 1 and 2, while One-Way Analysis of Variance (ANOVA) was utilized in Problem 4 and 5 as the statistical tools used in the study.

RESULTS, DISCUSSION, AND IMPLICATIONs

The results show that when the strands were taken as a whole (M=4.08, SD= 0.49), there is a High extent of application of ESP in the EAPP curriculum for the senior high in the Municipality of Binalbagan. However, when grouped according to each strand, HE (M=4.41, SD=0.46), ABM (M=4.35, SD=0.44), and HUMSS (M=4.30, SD=0.44) were of the Very High Extent. While GAS (M=3.89, SD=0.50), IA (M=3.85, SD=0.64), and AFA (M=3.69, SD=0.45) were of the High Extent. The results of the study are supported by Maa and Ouargla's study (2013) that many participants believed that the selected materials for their field rarely satisfy them that the materials are related to their future job needs. However, other respondents found the materials helpful to them. Hence, the topics related to the interest of the students have given them the general and relevant knowledge about the world of their chosen track (Rodríguez, 2014).

Moreover, when the strands were categorized by content standard, ABM (M=4.41, SD= 0.38), and HE (M=4.44, SD=0.47) were of the Very High Extent. However, HUMSS (M=4.26, SD=0.51), GAS (M=3.93, SD=0.50), IA (M=3.99, SD=0.54), and AFA (M=3.69, SD=0.48) were of the High Extent. The result is supported by Yang (2012) which stated that students perceive that the contents that they have are aligned and relevant to their chosen fields, and the needs are being met; thus, the texts help them to be socially participative beyond the classroom.

On the other hand, when the strands were categorized according to performance standard, HUMSS (M=4.34, SD=0.42), ABM (M=4.29, SD= 0.54), and HE (M=4.39, SD=0.52) were of the Very High Extent, while GAS (M=3.88, SD=0.58), IA (M=3.80, SD=0.73), and AFA (M= 3.69, SD=0.52) were of the High Extent. The results of the study showed a similarity on the study of Benavent and Sanchez-Reyes (2015) which stated that students do differentiated activities relevant to their target situation that can be done independently such as writing a report, filling out forms, preparing a presentation for a meeting and dealing with databases using English. Likewise, in the study of Barnawi (2011), students believe that the purpose of ESP program is to develop and enhance their four macro skills. Thus, the skill-based performance should be acquired, and it is more important than the specific language needed in the target situation (Hutchinson & Waters, 1987 as cited in Keefe, 2016).

There is a significant difference in the extent of application of ESP in the EAPP curriculum for the senior high in the public schools regarding the strands. The result of the study of Keefe (2016) showed that students' responses to the EAP program are positive in which the responses are congruent to the result of the present study.

Furthermore, to determine which among the strands created the significant difference, a Post Hoc test was applied. The result shows that significant difference was created between HUMSS and AFA, between ABM and AFA, and between ABM and GAS since their p-value ≤ 0.05. However, the findings on AFA and GAS show that the mean difference of the two strands are at below 0.05 level which revealed that there is an insufficiency on the learning and teaching materials intended for each strand in their EAPP class. Also, students are not well-motivated to their chosen strand due to the lessons and activities are given to them which they find uninteresting.

There is a significant difference in the extent of application of ESP in the EAPP curriculum among the strands when categorized according to content standard. The result of the study is supported by Ali and Salih (2013) as cited in Nguyen (2017) which stated that the inputs and the approach of the materials should be appropriate and relevant to the needs of the students that would meet the needs of the society. Moreover, Hyland (2002) as cited in Hyland (2012) stated that tasks and texts in every area of specialization vary to one another especially on learners' writing activities.

Since there is a significant difference, therefore a Post Hoc test was applied to determine which among the strands created a difference. A significant difference was created between HUMSS and AFA, between GAS and ABM, and between GAS and HE, since their p-value ≤ 0.05. However, AFA and ABM have negative mean differences in the extent of application of ESP. This result shows that the students were not able to receive the needed contents of their chosen strand. In contrary, the result of the study of Bhatia and Bremner (2012) revealed that there is a significant difference between the contents of the specialization that affect the teaching-learning discourse and have a direct implication for English courses. Further, Lasala (2014) stated that modules should include topics which are relevant to the communicative abilities since senior high students have an average communicative competence both in their oral and writing skills, but these could still be improved.

On the other hand, there is a significant difference in the extent of application of ESP in the EAPP curriculum among the strands when categorized according to performance standard. The result of the study is in agreement with the result of Jon Larsson's (2001) study as cited in Gavrilova and Trostina (2014) which revealed that there is a significant improvement on the communicative skills and social interaction ability of the learners regarding their Task-Based Language Learning.

Since there is a significant difference, therefore a Post Hoc test was applied to determine which among the strands created a difference. A significant difference was created between GAS and HE, between IA and HE, and between AFA and HE, since their p-value ≤ 0.05. According to Hyland (2002), as cited in Hyland (2012), the writing tasks of the students focus on their chosen field. Furthermore, Stan et al. (2013), the integration of English vocabulary and structures in meaningful contexts is a reinforcement of professional notion, concepts, and ideas that increase students' motivation. Moreover, students would start using what they learn and apply it to their professional work and studies. Hence, the ESP approach could enhance students' interest and motivation in their respective fields.

The high extent of application of ESP in the EAPP curriculum for the senior high in the public schools in the Municipality of Binalbagan indicates that students who acquire ESP strategies and materials on their EAPP class have a great chance to be competent and skilled individuals in their field of specialization. Likewise, the reading selections, lessons, differentiated activities, and ESP approaches, which are relevant and consistent with their strands, they have could give them the necessary knowledge and skills that they would encounter in their college, employment, or business. Moreover, the results regarding standards imply that the contents and competencies aligned to their chosen fields could be a factor for them to perform well when they are in their respective career.

However, using the Post Hoc test in determining which among the strands created a difference, the results reveal that there is no significant difference in AFA and GAS. The results indicate that students who enrolled in these strands are nearly prone to be insufficient on their knowledge and skills that are supposed to be expected when they are in their actual work or course. Likewise, there are no differences found in the assessment of the AFA, ABM, and HE when the Post Hoc test was utilized. The result indicates that the contents and tasks that were presented to the learners are not enough to meet their needs. Hence, learners would have struggled with learning the concepts of their chosen strands and accomplishing the responsibilities that require needed competencies.

CONCLUSIONS AND RECOMMENDATIONS

The result of the study reveals a high extent of application of ESP in the EAPP curriculum for the senior high in the public schools of Binalbagan. There are consistency and relevancy of the instructional materials, activities, and learning resources given to the students who belong to their chosen strand. Perhaps, the EAPP teachers integrate the ESP materials, methods, and approaches intended to the strands they are teaching with.

Moreover, there is a significant difference in the extent of application of ESP in the EAPP curriculum for the senior high in the public schools of Binalbagan. Thus, ESP is compliant to the GAS, IA, AFA, HUMSS, HE, and ABM students to acquire the necessary knowledge and to practice the necessary skills required in their field of specialization for the preparation for their future endeavor.

The curriculum designers must use the result of this study to design lessons and activities needed by every strand that will prepare students for their chosen courses for the college years. At the same time, it may use as a guide for the curriculum makers to include authentic and contextualized activities in medicine, business, academics, law, criminal education, tourism, and other fields of specialization.

The English Education Program Specialist (EEPS) must use the results as a guide to provide training for English teachers and to customize instructional materials in EAPP subject. Likewise, the results will use as the basis to conduct a needs assessment and to develop plans and programs for ESP teachers.

The school administrators must give focus on designing and contextualizing the lessons and activities for English for Academic and Professional Purposes (EAPP) subject. The results may be the basis for planning programs in school or in a community that will prepare students for their future professions.

The English teachers must initiate classroom-based activities and integrate lessons related to the chosen strand of the students. Likewise, the results shall be used by the English teachers to integrate the competencies from the purposive communication and to provide ESP materials based on the needs of the students through using differentiated materials as the springboard for the discussion and applying the necessary skills not only on the reading and writing but also on the listening and speaking skills.

The senior high school students must use the results to help them realize the importance of English in their chosen strand and future profession and help them develop and enhance their communication skills in academe and activities related to their tracks.

The stakeholders must collaborate with the senior high school students especially to those strands which are aligned with their given work opportunity when students will be deployed to their agency or company for training purposes.

The future researchers must use the results of the study as the bases to conduct their research work on the effectiveness of using ESP approach to involve language supervisors, college teachers, and other stakeholders.

REFERENCES

Antic, Z. (2016). Teacher Education in English for Special Purposes. *Acta Facultatis Medicae Naissensis; Nis, 33*(3), 211–215. https://doi.org/http://dx.doi.org/10.1515/afmnai-2016-0022

Barnawi, O. Z. (2011). *Examining formative evaluation of an English for Specific Purposes Program* (Ph.D.). Indiana University of Pennsylvania, United States -- Pennsylvania. Retrieved from https://search.proquest.com/docview/867369327/abstract/B2ADBEE64E4F45F2PQ/1

Benavent, G. T., & Sánchez-Reyes, S. (2015). Target Situation as a Key Element for ESP (Law Enforcement) Syllabus Design. *Procedia - Social and Behavioral Sciences, 173*(Supplement C), 143–148. https://doi.org/10.1016/j.sbspro.2015.02.044

Bhatia, V., Anthony, L., & Noguchi, J. (2011). ESP in the 21st century: ESP theory and application today. In *Proceedings of the JACET 50th Commemorative International Convention* (Vol. 143).

Bhatia, V. & Bremner, S. (2012). English for Business Communication

Bracaj, M. (2014). Teaching English for specific purposes and teacher training. *European Scientific Journal, ESJ, 10*(2).

DO 32, s. 2016 - Addendum to DepEd Order No. 3, S. 2016 (Hiring Guidelines for Senior High School (SHS) Teaching Positions Effective School Year (SY) 2016-2017) | Department of Education. (n.d.). Retrieved March 8, 2018, fromhttp://www.deped.gov.ph/or ders/do-32-s-2016

Gavrilova, E., & Trostina, K. (2014). Teaching English For Professional Purposes (Epp) Vs Content And Language Integrated Learning (Clil): The Case Of Plekhanov Russian University Of Economics (Prue). *European Scientific Journal, ESJ, 10*(10). Retrieved from http://eujournal.org/index.php/esj/articl e/view/3686

Hyland, K. (2012). The Handbook of English for Specific Purposes (pp. 95–113). https://doi.org/10.1002/9781118339855 .ch5

Keefe, K. (2016). *The impact of English for Academic Purposes (EAP) programs on international students' success in university courses.* University of British Columbia. https://doi.org/10.14288/1.0306924

Kuo, S. (2016). Assessing Tertiary-level ESP Enhancement Criteria for Ameliorating Occupational Mobility: Commerce and Industry Perceptions. *Theory and Practice in Language Studies; London, 6*(6), 1157–1165. http://dx.doi.org/10.17507/tpls.0606.04

Lasala, C. B. (2014). Communicative Competence of Secondary Senior Students: Language Instructional Pocket. *Procedia - Social and Behavioral Sciences, 134*(Supplement C), 226–237. https://doi.org/10.1016/j.sbspro.2014.0 4.243

Maa, M. H. M. S., & Ouargla, P. U. (2013). ESP Materials Selection.

Nguyen, T. C. N. (2017). *Aligning English for Specific Purposes (ESP) curriculum with industry needs: Language practices for Vietnam's globalised workplaces* (Thesis). Queensland University of Technology. Retrieved from https://eprints.qut.edu.au/110536/

Paltridge, B., & Starfield, S. (Eds.). (2013). *The handbook of English for specific purposes.* Malden, Ma: John Wiley & Sons Inc.

Rodríguez, G. L. A. (2014). Reading Through ESP in an Undergraduate Law Program. *Profile; Bogota, 16*(1), 105–118.

Ruiz-Garrido, M. F., Palmer, J. C., & Fortanet-gomez, I. (2010). *English for Professional and Academic Purposes.* Rodopi.

Senior High School | Department of Education. (n.d.). Retrieved March 8, 2018, from http://www.deped.gov.ph/k-to-12/faq/senior-high-school

SHS Student Primer_Colored LowRes.pdf. (n.d.). Retrieved November 19, 2017, from http://www.deped.gov.ph/sites/default/f iles/SHS%20Student%20Primer_Color ed%20LowRes.pdf

Stan, R. S., Oroian, E., Moanga, A., Adam, S., & Mihai, M. (2013). English for Specific Purposes - a Stimulating and Innovative Approach for Agricultural Universities. *Bulletin of University of Agricultural Sciences and Veterinary Medicine Cluj-Napoca. Horticulture, 69*(2). https://doi.org/10.15835/buasvmcn-hort:8840

Yang, W. (2012). A Study of Students' Perceptions and Attitudes towards Genre-based ESP Writing Instruction. Asian ESP Journal